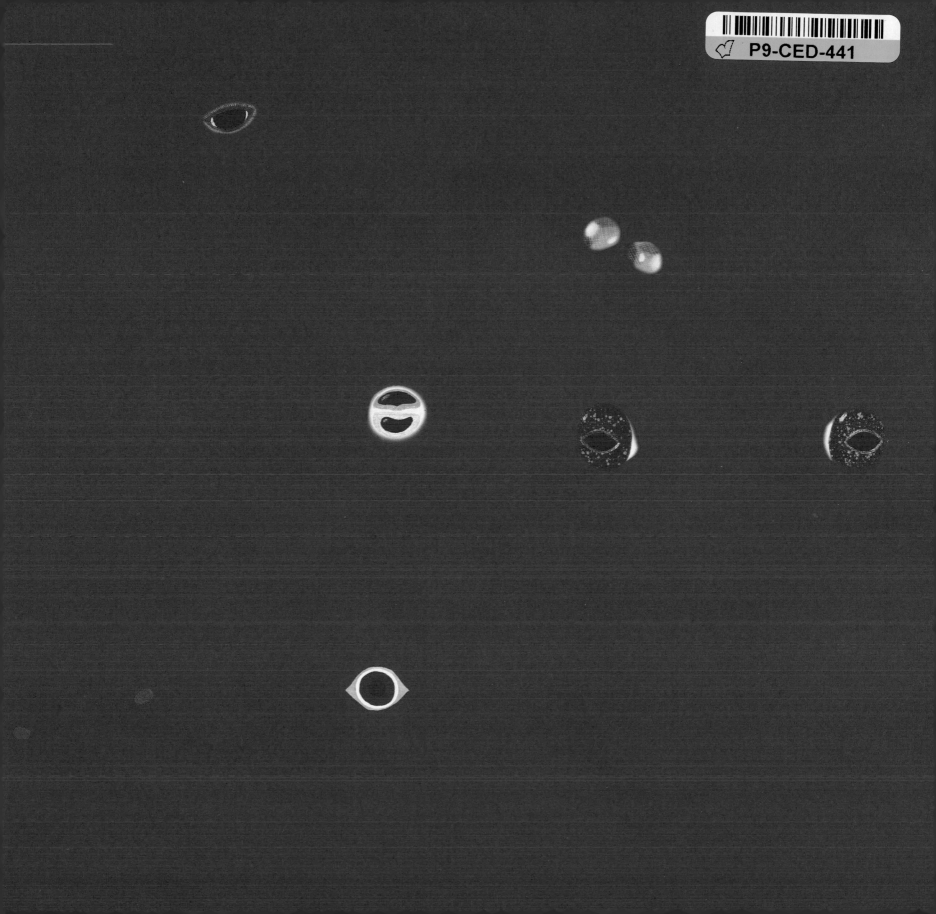

I've Got Eyes!

To Sue. –J.M.

For Morgan & Elliot. –H.T.

Text copyright © 2018 Julie Murphy • Illustrations copyright © 2018 Hannah Tolson

Published in 2018 by Amicus Ink, an imprint of Amicus • P.O. Box 1329 • Mankato, MN 56002 • www.amicuspublishing.us

Names: Murphy, Julie, author. | Tolson, Hannah, illustrator.

Title: I've got eyes! : exceptional eyes of the animal world / by Julie Murphy ; illustrated by Hannah Tolson.

Other titles: I have got eyes! | Exceptional eyes of the animal world

Description: Mankato, MN : Amicus/Amicus Ink. [2018] | Audience: K to grade 3.

Identifiers: LCCN 2017049013 | ISBN 9781681524047 (hardcover)

Subjects: LCSH: Eye--Juvenile literature. | Physiology--Juvenile literature. | Anatomy--Juvenile literature. | Animals--Adaptation--Juvenile literature.

Classification: LCC QL949 .M87 2018 | DDC 591.4/4--dc23

LC record available at https://lccn.loc.gov/2017049013

Editor: Rebecca Glaser

Designer: Veronica Scott

First edition 9 8 7 6 5 4 3 2 1 • Printed in China

I'VE GOT EYES!

EXCEPTIONAL EYES OF THE ANIMAL WORLD

BY JULIE MURPHY • ILLUSTRATED BY HANNAH TOLSON

amicus ink

Mankato, Minnesota

Eyes blink, stare, hide, and scare.
But most of all, eyes SEE.

Some have eight eyes, lots have two . . .
let's SEE what creatures' eyes can do!

I've got BIG, BULGING eyes.

Each of my eyes is about as
big as my brain!

The TARSIER'S oversized eyes are perfect for finding tasty insects in the jungle at night.

I've got SHARP eyes.

My eyes can spot
my next meal from
a mile away!

The PEREGRINE FALCON'S forward-facing eyes see other birds in the distance and judge how far away they are. One swoop later, and it's lunchtime.

I've got OBLONG eyes.

My wide eyes make
sure no one creeps
up on me!

The long, rectangle-shaped pupils in a GOAT'S eyes give a broad view of the land. This lets the goat watch for predators while it eats.

I've got HIDING eyes.

Lacy flaps of skin over my eyes are the finishing touch to my clever disguise.

The CROCODILE FISH hides from predators by looking like its surroundings. Its eyes must be hidden too, or the fish could be noticed.

I've got SOLO eyes.

My eyes can work alone,
with each one looking in
a different direction.

The CHAMELEON'S eyes see only a tiny pin-hole view of the world. Having two views is twice as good when hunting for insects and avoiding hungry birds and snakes.

I've got BLINKING eyes.

My eyes blink to help me eat!

When a FROG blinks, its eyeballs sink down into its head. This pushes food from the mouth into the throat.

I've got HANDLEBAR eyes.

My eyes are on long stalks, like a bike's handlebars. They improve my view and make me look good too!

Male STALK-EYED FLIES with the longest
eyestalks get the widest view of their world.
They also get the most females as mates!

I've got DESERT-PROOF eyes.

My eyes are not bothered
by scratchy sand stirred
up by the desert wind.

Each of the CAMEL'S eyes has two rows of eyelashes and three eyelids to keep out dust and sand. It's like having built-in goggles!

I've got DOUBLE-DECKER eyes.

My eyes poke up as
I float at the surface.
Few fish watch above
water like me!

The FOUR-EYED FISH really has just two eyes, but each has two parts. The top halves see in air, while the bottom halves watch underwater.

I've got EIGHT eyes.

Six in front, and one more on each side make eight. My eyes have got you covered!

The WOLF SPIDER has excellent night vision to find and chase down prey or ambush it as it passes by.

I've got ODD eyes.

My two eyes are very
different from each other
because they do very
different jobs.

The COCK-EYED SQUID has a big yellow eye that spots animal shapes in the sunlit waters above.

Its small blue eye watches for glow-in-the-dark animals in the murky depths below.

I've got WRAP-AROUND eyes.

My eyes could still be watching you even after I've passed by!

The DRAGONFLY's two huge compound eyes are made of thousands of smaller ones. They all point different ways, looking everywhere at once—even backwards!

I've got BLIND eyes.

My eyes cannot see. They are covered by skin.

The OLM lives in total
darkness, deep inside caves.

Even working eyes are useless there!
This sightless cave salamander finds
its food by smell and taste.

You've got eyes too!
What can your eyes do?

cock-eyed squid

goat

chameleon

wolf spider

crocodile fish

tarsier